Where in the World Can I . . .

CLIMB A TOWER?

Where in the World Can I . . .

CLIMB A TOWER?

www.worldbook.com

World Book, Inc.
180 North LaSalle Street, Suite 900
Chicago, Illinois 60601
USA

For information about other World Book publications, visit our website at **www.worldbook.com** or call **1-800-WORLDBK (967-5325).**

For information about sales to schools and libraries, call 1-800-975-3250 (United States), or 1-800-837-5365 (Canada).

Library of Congress Cataloging-in-Publication Data for this volume has been applied for.

Where in the World Can I...
ISBN: 978-0-7166-2178-2 (set, hc.)

Climb a Tower?
ISBN: 978-0-7166-2180-5 (hc.)

Also available as:
ISBN: 978-0-7166-2190-4 (e-book)

STAFF

Writer: Shawn Brennan

Executive Committee
President
Jim O'Rourke

Vice President and Editor in Chief
Paul A. Kobasa

Vice President, Finance
Donald D. Keller

Vice President, Marketing
Jean Lin

Vice President, International Sales
Maksim Rutenberg

Vice President, Technology
Jason Dole

Director, Human Resources
Bev Ecker

Editorial
Director, New Print
Tom Evans

Managing Editor, New Print
Jeff De La Rosa

Senior Editor, New Print
Shawn Brennan

Editor, New Print
Grace Guibert

Librarian
S. Thomas Richardson

Manager, Contracts & Compliance (Rights & Permissions)
Loranne K. Shields

Manager, Indexing Services
David Pofelski

Digital
Director, Digital Product Development
Erika Meller

Manager, Digital Produc
Jonathan Wills

Graphics and Design
Senior Art Director
Tom Evans

Coordinator, Design Development and Production
Brenda Tropinski

Media Researcher
Rosalia Bledsoe

Manufacturing/ Production
Manufacturing Manager
Anne Fritzinger

Proofreader
Nathalie Strassheim

TABLE OF CONTENTS

WHAT IS A TOWER?

A tower is a building that is much taller than it is wide or thick. Towers are generally taller than other buildings around them. They may stand alone or be attached to walls or buildings. The first towers were used for military or religious purposes. Over the centuries, towers have been used for other things.

Towers were rare in ancient times. One of the most famous ancient towers was the Lighthouse of Alexandria, Egypt. It was built in the 200's B.C.

During the Middle Ages in Europe (about the A.D. 400's through the 1400's), people built towers along the walls of castles and cities. The towers helped the people keep a lookout and defend the walls. Later, many Europeans built slender bell towers on their city halls.

Towers can be important religious buildings. *Buddhists (BUD ihsts* or *BOO dihsts)* build towers called *pagodas (puh GOH duhz)*. Buddhists practice the religion called *Buddhism (BUD ihz uhm* or *BOO dihz uhm)*.

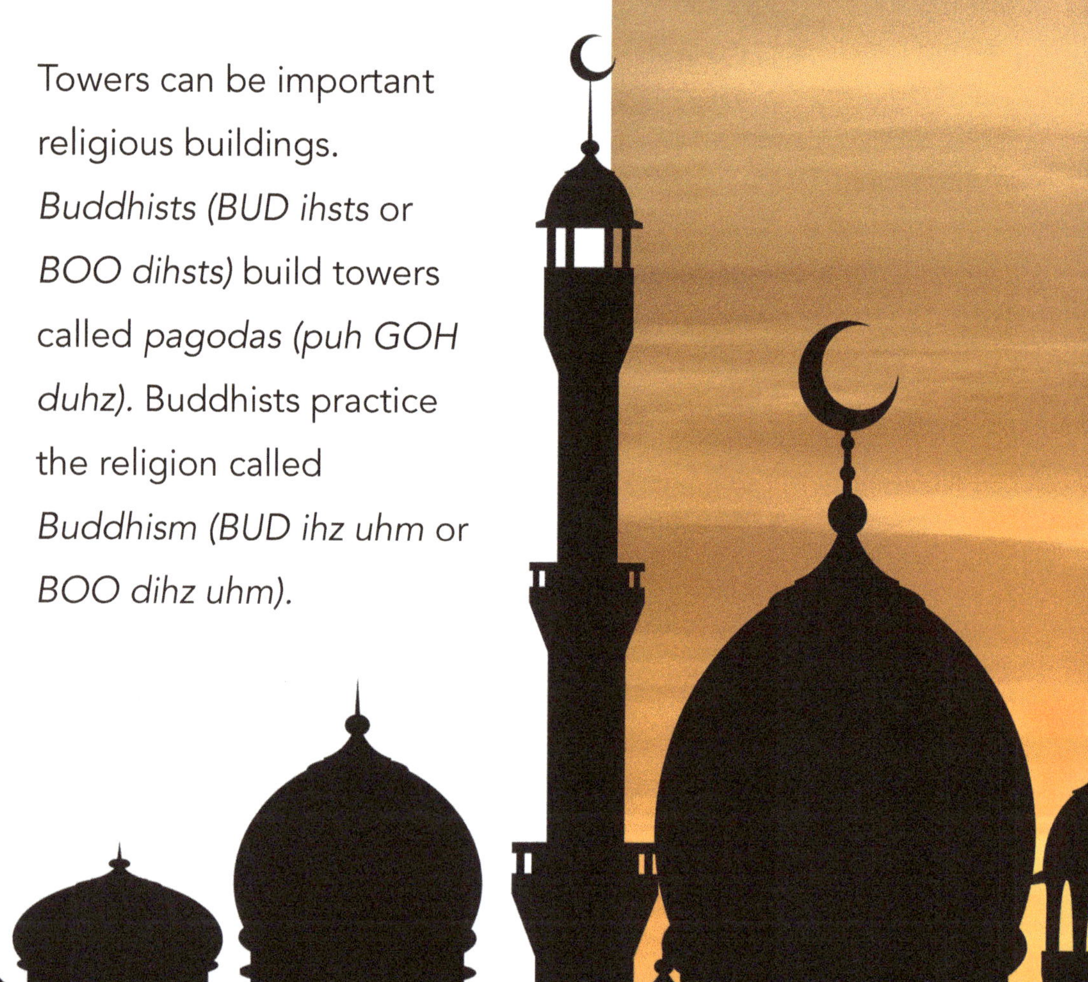

Muslims are called to prayer from a tower called a *minaret (mihn uh REHT* or *MIHN uh reht)*. Muslims are people who follow the faith of Islam *(IHS luhm, IHZ lum,* or *ihs LAHM)*.

Today, towns use water towers to store water. Holding the water up high creates pressure for piping it to homes and businesses. Broadcasting towers hold radio or TV antennas *(an TEHN uhz).* An *antenna* is a rod that receives or sends television and radio signals. Skyscrapers are also a kind of tower. Skyscrapers are designed mainly for people to live and work in. Towers are not usually used for people to live in.

Towers and other buildings are designed and planned by people called architects *(AHR kuh tehkts)* and engineers. Architects try to design a building to meet people's needs, look attractive, and last a long time. They make room for all the things people will do in the building. They make sure it is the right size and shape. They choose building materials that look good and wear well. They design strong walls and *foundations* (bottom parts). Engineers use science to plan and help construct buildings.

Have you ever wanted to climb a tower? You can climb very high inside some famous towers and look out to see a spectacular view. In some very tall towers, you can even step outside on a ledge or even jump from high above! Some of these towers are new and some are very old.

LET'S EXPLORE SOME OF THESE TOWERS!

THE GIRALDA

The Giralda *(hee RAHL dah)* is the bell tower of the cathedral of Seville *(suh VIHL)*. Seville is a city in the southern part of Spain. The Giralda is the city's symbol. The tower was once a Muslim minaret. It stands over 300 feet (91 meters) high. It was built in the 1100's. The Giralda is important because it is a fine example of the blend of different cultures that defines Spain.

Seville Cathedral is the third largest cathedral in the world. A *cathedral* is the official church of a bishop. Seville Cathedral is also the largest Gothic *(GAHTH ihk)* cathedral in the world. *Gothic* architecture is a style that developed from the mid-1100's to about 1400. Gothic churches are very large, tall churches known for their arched ceilings and towers. The Giralda tower and the Seville Cathedral are the most visited monuments in Seville.

The cathedral stands where there once was a Moorish mosque. Moors, Muslims from northwestern Africa, lived in Seville for hundreds of years. In the 1200's, the Moors left, and the mosque was made into a church. The Gothic cathedral was built between 1402 and 1519. It holds the tombs of Ferdinand III and Christopher Columbus. Ferdinand III was a king who ruled much of Spain during the 1200's. Columbus was an Italian explorer who became famous for sailing west across the Atlantic Ocean in 1492.

Around 1400, Christians placed a cross and a bell on top of the tower. During the 1500's, a section was added to the tower to include more bells. A bronze statue of a woman was added to the top of the bell tower.

The statue is 13 feet (4 meters) tall. It represents the Christian faith. It is called the *Giraldillo* *(HEE rahl DEE oh)*, which means *weather vane* in Spanish.

The statue turns to show the direction of the wind. It is from this statue that the Giralda takes its name.

You can climb the bell tower up a 34-story ramp. The slope decreases as you reach the top. The ramps were built to fit horses and riders. Muslim worshippers rode to the top of the mosque five times a day to pray.

When you climb to the top, you will be rewarded with a beautiful view of Seville! Take your time and enjoy the views of the orange trees in the courtyard. You will also see the cathedral's gargoyles *(GAHR goylz)* and slender spires. A gargoyle is a decorated waterspout that sticks out of a building. It is a carving of a figure that is part animal and part human.

Giralda tower and Seville Cathedral are part of a group of buildings that includes the Alcázar *(AL kuh zahr)* palace and the Archive of the Indies. The Alcázar was originally built in the 900's as the palace of the Muslim governor. It was rebuilt many times. The Alcázar is used today as the Spanish royal family's home in Seville. It is one of the most beautiful palaces in Spain. The Archive was built in 1585. It houses documents about the colonization of the Americas.

In 1987, the United Nations Educational, Scientific and Cultural Organization (UNESCO) made the Giralda, along with Seville Cathedral, the Alcázar, and the Archive of the Indies, a World Heritage Site. Some of these places are special because of the plants and animals that live there. Others are special because of events in history that happened at them. Governments are required to preserve and protect World Heritage Sites.

OTHER TOWERS TO CLIMB

LEANING TOWER OF PISA

Another interesting tower in Europe you can climb is the famous Leaning Tower of Pisa *(PEE zuh)*. Pisa is an old city in central Italy. It lies on the Arno River in the Tuscany *(TUHS kuh nee)* region. The city is about 6 miles (10 kilometers) east of the Ligurian *(lih GYOO rih uhn)* Sea. The tower leans because it was built on soil that was not firm.

The tower is a church bell tower. It is one of three buildings that make up the cathedral of Pisa. These buildings are known for their colorful marble and beautiful arches. The tower is 51 feet (15.5 meters) in diameter and about 180 feet (55 meters) tall. The tower has eight floors. Each floor has arches all the way around it. You can climb the inner staircase of almost 300 steps to the top!

People began building the tower more than 800 years ago and finished it almost 200 years later. After the first three floors were built, the tower began to sink and lean over.

Each year, the tower leaned a little more. It leaned 14 ½ feet (4.4 meters) out of line from the seventh story!

According to *legend* (an old story), the Italian physicist Galileo *(gal uh LAY oh* or *gal uh LEE oh)* made famous experiments by dropping weights from the tower in 1589. Galileo was born in Pisa. He is supposed to have gone to the top of the tower with two cannon balls. One ball was large and the other was small. He dropped them both at the same time. They reached the ground at nearly the same time. There was a small difference, but not nearly so great as the difference between their weights.

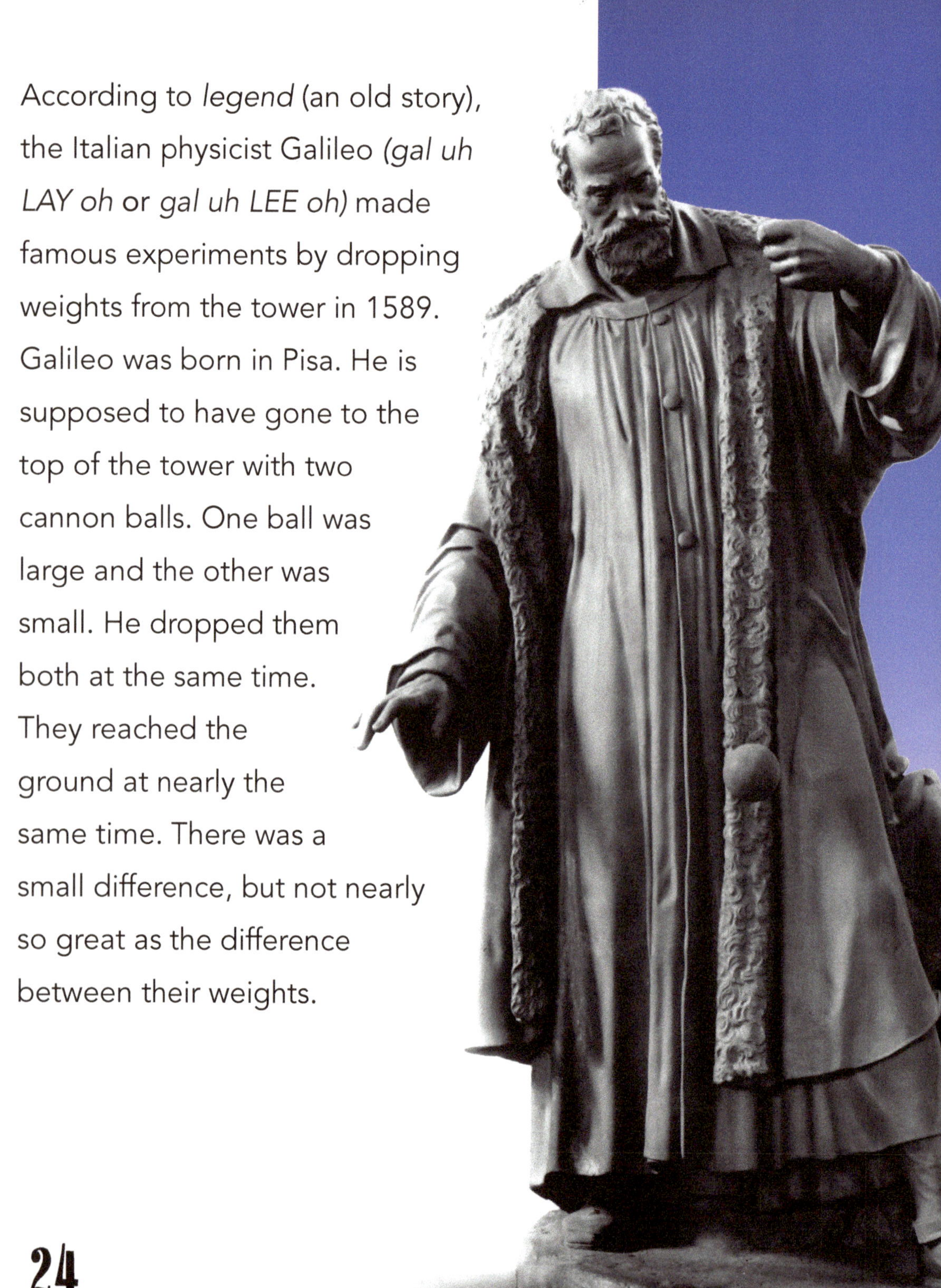

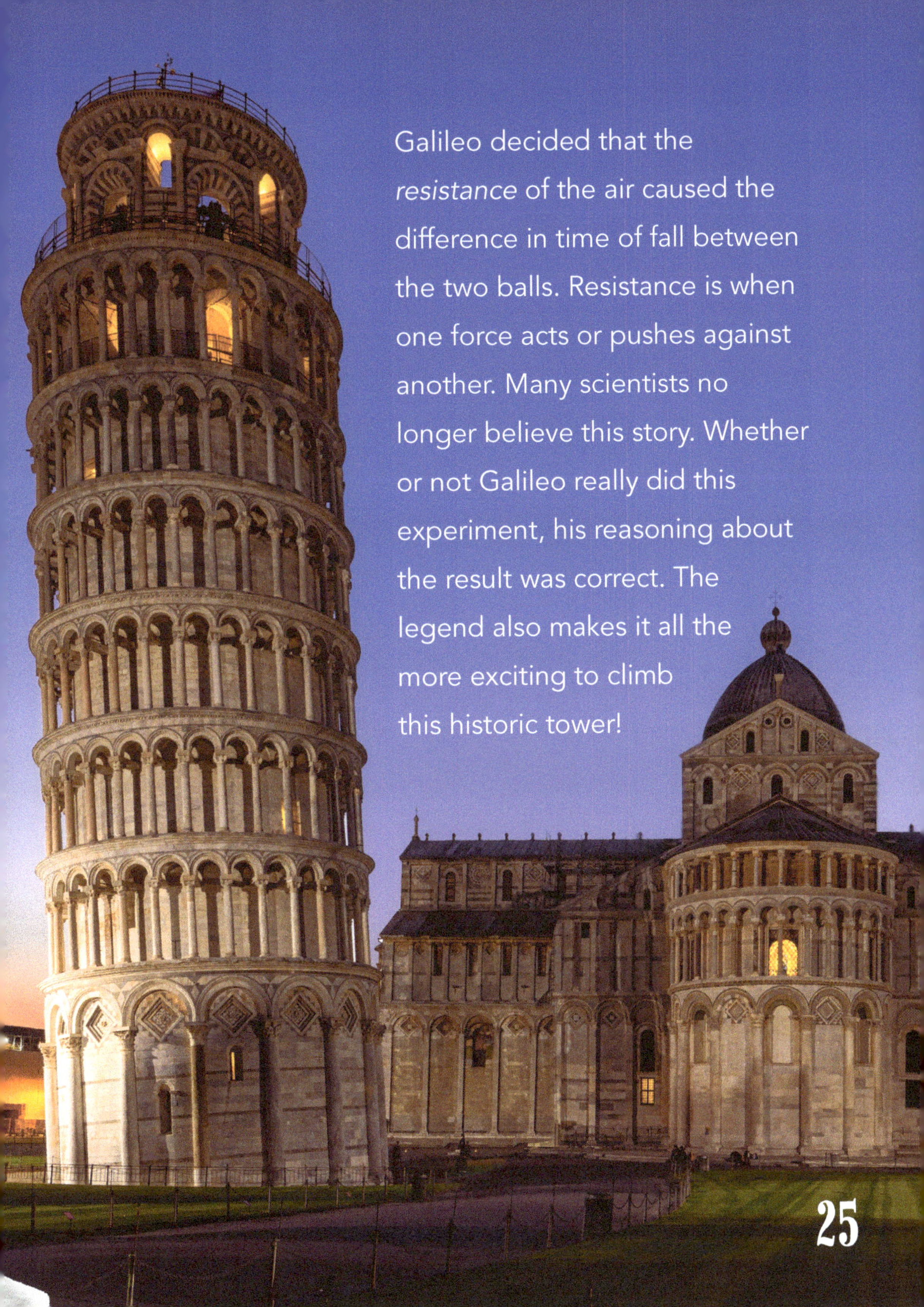

Galileo decided that the *resistance* of the air caused the difference in time of fall between the two balls. Resistance is when one force acts or pushes against another. Many scientists no longer believe this story. Whether or not Galileo really did this experiment, his reasoning about the result was correct. The legend also makes it all the more exciting to climb this historic tower!

In 1987, UNESCO made the Piazza del Duomo *(pee AZ uh dehl DWAW moh),* which includes the tower, a World Heritage Site. *(Duomo* is the Italian word for *cathedral.)*

In 1990, the tower was closed for repairs. Engineers worked on the tower's foundation. They straightened the tower enough to keep it from falling. The tower opened again in June 2001.

STATUE OF LIBERTY

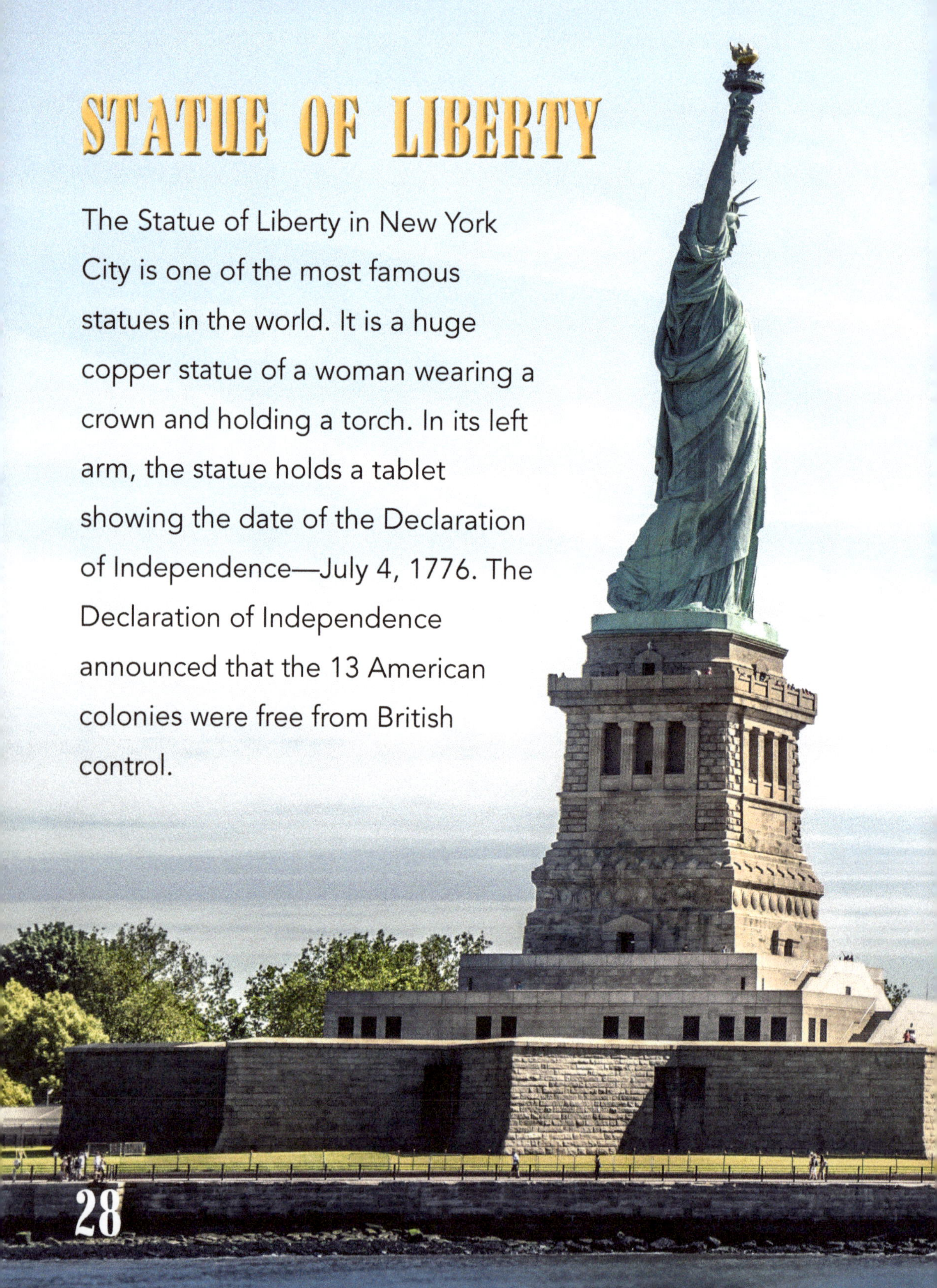

The Statue of Liberty in New York City is one of the most famous statues in the world. It is a huge copper statue of a woman wearing a crown and holding a torch. In its left arm, the statue holds a tablet showing the date of the Declaration of Independence—July 4, 1776. The Declaration of Independence announced that the 13 American colonies were free from British control.

The statue stands on Liberty Island in New York Harbor. It has come to be a symbol of the United States. The Statue of Liberty attracts visitors from all over the world. But did you know that it is really a tower? Inside the statue are two stairways. You can climb to the crown and look out through one of 25 windows!

The statue stands 151 feet (46 meters) high from its feet to the top of the torch. It weighs 225 tons (204 metric tons). The statue stands atop a *pedestal* (base support). The pedestal is 89 feet (27 meters) tall. It rests on a huge concrete foundation 65 feet (20 meters) tall. You can climb 192 steps to the top of the pedestal. Then you can climb 354 steps from the statue's heels to the crown. That is about the height of a 20-story building!

The torch towers 305 feet 1 inch (92.99 meters) above the base of the monument. At night, its gold-covered flame glows with light from 16 powerful lamps arranged around the rim of the torch. Lamps shining up from below light up the rest of the statue.

The people of France gave the Statue of Liberty to the people of the United States in 1884. This gift was an expression of friendship and of the ideal of liberty shared by both peoples. French citizens donated the money for the statue to be built.

People in the United States raised the funds to construct the foundation and the pedestal. The French sculptor Frédéric Auguste Bartholdi *(fray day REEK oh GOOST bahr tawl DEE* or *bahr THOL dee)* designed the statue and chose its site. The statue was dedicated by U.S. President Grover Cleveland in 1886.`

Gustave Eiffel *(goos TAV EYE fuhl)*, a French engineer, designed the framework that supports the statue's copper covering. Eiffel later built the famous Eiffel Tower in Paris. The framework for the Statue of Liberty is much like what he later used for the Eiffel Tower. The Statue of Liberty consists of a central tower of four iron columns that go up and down. These are connected by beams that go straight across and from corner to corner. Iron supporting beams leading up and out from the tower support the statue's raised right arm

In 1924, the Statue of Liberty became a national monument. The National Park Service took over responsibility for maintaining the statue in 1933. In 1965, Ellis Island became part of the monument. Ellis Island served as a reception center for immigrants for more than 60 years, until 1954. In 1984, UNESCO made the Statue of Liberty a World Heritage Site.

Major repairs and renovation were carried out for the 1986 centenary (100th anniversary) of the Statue of Liberty. A new flame was built that more faithfully matches the design of Liberty's original flame. The surface of the statue was cleaned, its framework repaired, and new elevators added. The ventilation system was also improved. The statue was reopened on July 4, 1986.

EIFFEL TOWER

The Eiffel Tower is the most famous building in Paris. It stands in a beautiful park called the Champ de Mars *(SHOM doo MAHS)* near the Seine *(sayn)* River. The building includes restaurants and decks people can stand on to look down on the city and surrounding areas.

The tower rises 984 feet (300 meters) above the ground. You can climb 704 steps to the tower's second level. Here, you can wander around the center of the tower's metal structure. You will also have a breathtaking view of Paris all around you!

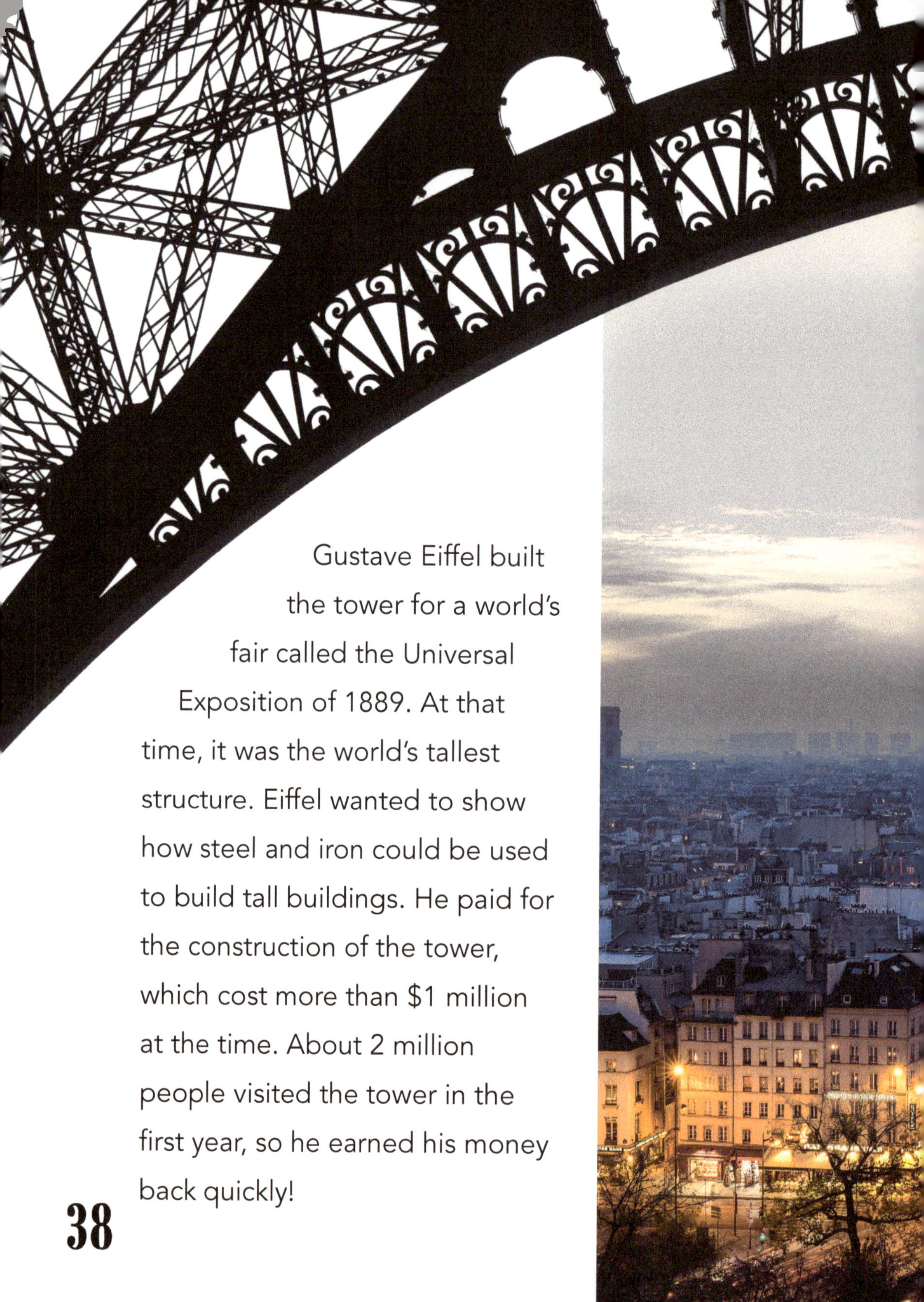

Gustave Eiffel built the tower for a world's fair called the Universal Exposition of 1889. At that time, it was the world's tallest structure. Eiffel wanted to show how steel and iron could be used to build tall buildings. He paid for the construction of the tower, which cost more than $1 million at the time. About 2 million people visited the tower in the first year, so he earned his money back quickly!

In 1991, UNESCO made the banks of the Seine River a World Heritage Site. The area includes the Eiffel Tower as well as the Louvre *(loov* or *LOO vruh)* art museum, the Place de la Concorde *(PLAHS duh lah kon KAWRD)* (Square of Peace), the Grand *(grahn)* and Petit Palais *(puh TEE pah LAY)* exhibition hall and museum complex, the Cathedral of Notre Dame *(noh truh DAHM)*, and the Sainte-Chapelle *(SAHNT shah PEHL)* royal chapel.

OUT ON A LEDGE!

THE LEDGE

There are some towers where you can explore the *outside* of the building from high above! You can walk out on the Ledge of the Willis Tower in Chicago, Illinois, in the United States. Here you can view downtown and beyond from a glass box 1,353 feet (412 meters) above the street! The boxes extend out 4 3⁄10 feet (1.3 meters) from the skyscraper's Skydeck on the 103rd floor. On a clear day, visitors can see four states—Illinois, Indiana, Michigan, and Wisconsin!

The Willis Tower is one of the tallest buildings in the United States. It has 110 stories, reaching 1,450 feet (442 meters) high. Antenna towers on top of the Willis Tower bring the total height to 1,707 feet (520 meters). The Willis Tower was built by Sears, Roebuck and Co. It was built between 1970 and 1974.

THE EDGEWALK

In downtown Toronto, Ontario, in Canada, you can be attached to a harness and take the world's highest "hands-free" walk on the CN Tower! The tower's EdgeWalk allows visitors to walk along a 5-foot- (1.5-meter-) wide ledge that encircles the top of the structure's main *pod* (rounded section). This is at a height of 1,168 feet (356 meters)! Don't look down!

The CN Tower is the tallest structure in the Western Hemisphere. It stands 1,815 feet 5 inches (553.33 meters) high. The building has a tapered shape like a needle. It is made of concrete and steel. The CN Tower has become one of the most familiar landmarks in Canada. The tower was built by the Canadian National Railway Company and opened in 1976.

THE SKYWALK AND SKYJUMP

In Auckland, New Zealand, you can take a stroll on the SkyWalk and see the city from 630 feet (192 meters) above!

You will be harnessed to a ledge on the country's tallest building, the Sky Tower. The Sky Tower is 1,076 feet (328 meters) tall. It is the tallest freestanding structure in the Southern Hemisphere. The Sky Tower was built between 1994 and 1997.

If that's not "edgy" enough for you, take a flying leap! You can do just that on the Sky Tower's SkyJump. You will be strapped to the building with a springy bungee *(BUHN jee)* cord. You can then hurl yourself down at 53 miles (85 kilometers) an hour!

Wheeeeeeeee!

Now that you've read about these amazing structures, which tower would you like to climb? Why? Read on to find some books and websites that tell you more about towers and how they are built.

BOOKS AND WEBSITES

BOOKS

Building Structures and Towers by Tammy Enz (Heinemann-Raintree, 2017)
This book uses engaging text and hands-on projects to help young readers explore real-life structure and tower engineering projects, including the science behind how these buildings are planned and built.

Skyscrapers by Libby Romero (National Geographic Society, 2017)
Learn all about the world's most amazing skyscrapers—from the first, to the tallest, to how they're built, and everything in between—in this National Geographic Kids book.

Skyscrapers and Towers by Shirley Duke (Rourke, 2015)
Presents materials and design techniques used to counter such forces as wind speed, gravity, and weight to make these buildings structurally sound, along with sustainable designs that allow them to be built higher and higher. Includes a timeline, glossary, list of websites, and comprehension questions.

WEBSITES

Inventors of Tomorrow – Towers: Engineering for Kids
https://inventorsoftomorrow.com/2016/09/21/engineering-towers-2/

This site is packed with fun, easy, play-tested STEM enrichment activities for kids. Include art projects, crafts, recommended songs, games, book reviews, science experiments, building projects, free printable worksheets, and posters.

Science Kids
http://www.sciencekids.co.nz/sciencefacts/engineering/buildings.html

Facts about famous buildings and skyscrapers around the world.

Skyscraper Page
http://skyscraperpage.com/

This website provides information on skyscrapers and buildings around the world.

INDEX

ACKNOWLEDGMENTS

Cover: © Aleksandar Georgiev, iStockphoto
2-3 © Paop/Dreamstime
5 © Michal Stipek, Shutterstock
6-7 World Book illustrations by Birney Lettick; © Shutterstock
8-9 © Shutterstock
10-11 © Chyrko Olena, Shutterstock; © Andrew Watson, Getty Images
12-13 © Shutterstock
14-15 Alejandro Guichot (licensed under CC BY 3.0); Carlos Teixidor Cadenas (licensed under CC BY-SA 4.0)
16-23 © Shutterstock
24-25 © Ekaterinabelova/Dreamstime; © SSPL/Getty Images
26-29 © Shutterstock
30-31 © Don Emmert, AFP/Getty Images; National Park Service
32-33 World Book illustration by Zorica Dabich; © Black Star/Alamy Images; © Shutterstock
34-35 © Spencer Platt, Getty Images
36-37 © Matthew Dixon, Shutterstock; © BSIP SA/Alamy Images
38-39 © Shutterstock; © Alex Trofimova, iStockphoto
40-41 © Richard Ellis, Alamy Images; © Turtix/Shutterstock
42-43 © Tom Szczerbowski, Getty Images; © Shutterstock
44-45 © Matiascausa/Shutterstock

www.ingramcontent.com/pod-product-compliance
Ingram Content Group UK Ltd.
Pitfield, Milton Keynes, MK11 3LW, UK
UKHW061951290726
14090UKWH00021B/1180